Some Unsayable Blue

poems by

Susan Sample

Finishing Line Press
Georgetown, Kentucky

Some Unsayable Blue

Copyright © 2019 by Susan Sample
ISBN 978-1-63534-977-1 First Edition
All rights reserved under International and Pan-American Copyright Conventions. No part of this book may be reproduced in any manner whatsoever without written permission from the publisher, except in the case of brief quotations embodied in critical articles and reviews.

ACKNOWLEDGMENTS

Grateful acknowledgement is made to the editors of the journals in which the following poems first appeared and to contest judges:

Intima: A Journal of Narrative Medicine: "Indigo"

TQ 11: "Coming to Terms"

"Bluing" received honorable mention in the 2017 *Writer's Digest* Poetry Awards.

My sincere thanks to Lisa Bickmore, Kimberly Johnson, Paisley Rekdal, Natasha Sajé, and Jennifer Tonge who continue to mentor me in the art and craft of poetry. Gratitude to Cindy Fazzi and Kate Woodworth for their unwavering friendship and support through the years, and to Scott Dalgarno for his insights into faith and grace.

Special thanks and gratitude to all of my family—my husband, daughters, cousins, sisters-in-law, brothers-in-law, sons-in-law, and stepmother—who accompanied me with love and understanding. And most of all, with love to my sister, Cari Ann Sample Malver.

Publisher: Leah Maines
Editor: Christen Kincaid
Cover Art: *Tree Life Cyanotype*, Sarah May, www.sarahlizmay.com
Author Photo: Sean Graff, seangraff.com
Cover Design: Leah Huete

Printed in the USA on acid-free paper.
Order online: www.finishinglinepress.com
also available on amazon.com

Author inquiries and mail orders:
Finishing Line Press
P. O. Box 1626
Georgetown, Kentucky 40324
U. S. A.

Table of Contents

Indigo 1

Bluing 2

Chicago Marathon: Remix 3

Coming to Terms 4

Guess Work 6

Sky Atlas 7

Center of Gravity 8

Last Rites 10

Ascension 18

Chromatics 21

After Blue 29

In memory of my father,

Malcolm Earl "Buck" Sample

"…Because it is *not* a question of an experience but of the *imagination*, always after the fact, always imminent."

—*Paul Ricoeur,* Living Up to Death

INDIGO

Backstroke is my strength, I tell myself, pulling
the raft's oars into my chest with a single, strong
motion. Cliffs rising from the river loom pale
as clouds cut through with dark swaths of coal.
Days later on the hospital's fourth floor,
black marbled linoleum is worn through
on the threshold of patient rooms. The mass is darker
on the X-ray of her lung, my friend tells me.
The second bag of vancomycin drips silently
through her IV; ice packs balanced
where her breast was. It's not as quiet
farther west in a chemotherapy suite
of pic lines, Hickmans, and ports. I listen
to the rhythm of Rituxan infusing my father.
The slow drip clicks like an aperture set for a long exposure:
one sleeve of his favorite fleece rolled up. He calls it
blue, though it is navy, or cobalt, grayer
than the quilt the nurse unfurls from a basket
to cover him with a hundred tiny squares tied with yarn
azure—yes, *l'zur*—not the weighted blue of the bowl
he ate cereal from as a boy that I found on the shelf
in his apartment this morning. I took it down and
rocked it in my hands, watching waves of glaze glisten
in sunlight or tears, I won't be able to remember.

BLUING

From the plane, I trace lines of winter:
the lake breaks into icy shards,
silver ridges edge mountains, peaks
pure white surge into significance

that dissolves with the shift of my eye.
Clouds rise higher, wider; white bands
stretch into translucence until they, too,
blur into the impenetrable blue horizon.

My jaw unclenches. In the face
of the inscrutable sky, muscles throughout my body
let go. There is no movement, no narrative
required of me until I land.

Is this what my dad sees outside his window?
I remember him last month stretched out
on his gray-blue recliner, wearing a blue shirt,
the only color at ninety-four he chooses:

blue bowl for oatmeal, blue spread covering
the rented hospice bed. Is there tranquility
living in one spectrum of light? Visible
only to those who live their dying?

CHICAGO MARATHON: REMIX

Lyrics from "Alive" by Empire of the Sun

They're running by me, alive, alive
People, thousands running
Running, running:
You make me feel so alive, alive

Speakers on the sidewalk
Cups of Gatorade, hundreds
Hundreds line the tables

Can you describe to me
All the world that you see?
Oh, I need it so much—

Drag queen in the red tutu
Winks, blows me a kiss,
Freedom is within you, Girl!

Stopping, leaning on the barricade
Sun warms my back
A borrowed black fleece

...World slows down as it goes...

Goodbye to last night:
Phone call in the taxi
Dad's in the hospital again
Thousand miles away, away

Say hello to the future

I can't, don't want to
Ever leave, leave. Just stay
here on the sideline
Loving every minute
So alive, alive
Alive, alive

COMING TO TERMS

I'm heading home.

I'm reading "situations of vertiginous vulnerability" penned by a woman with ovarian cancer.

I'm highlighting in pencil: *"...reading isn't the opposite of doing; it's the opposite of dying."*

I'm seated in the emergency exit row.

"...words will tell you things you never thought or felt before"

I'm balancing a yellow pad on my lap, scanning the sky between lines: *need copy of power of medical attorney, call re: commode, Citibank, cost of single room, cemetery.*

Only haze as we ascend. For days, fires have been burning to the north and south.

I want the blue of cruising altitude.

The second day of my visit, I wore a blouse intense as a desert's cloudless sky. "That's blue" was all my dad said.

I'm still worrying the image of him from the day before: dressed completely in shades of brown—an unfamiliar shirt of autumn plaid, dark slacks, belt, socks, and slip-on shoes.

Brown is opposite blue on the wheel of complementary colors. *Complementary brings perfection*, I read once. Paint a disc in equal parts with complementary colors, rotate it rapidly, and it will transform into whitish light.

"I'm in a fragile place," my dad said when I asked, tentatively—

The warning on the wing outside my window: "Do Not Step."

—I couldn't say it. He nodded to *anxious* and *uncertainty* when I offered possibilities, then added, "I'm glad you visited."

I'm the one *leaving*. I'm the one *passing*.

I wonder about the ethics of euphemism; the etymology of *provisional*? When does the future replace the time being?

I'm leaning forward, trying one last time to glimpse the Pacific, just a patch to remember, to place over my mind's eye when the plane inevitably turns inland.

All I can make out is the coastline. Not the rich denseness of earth, the unfathomable depth of water; just miles and miles of violent surf, exquisitely, sublimely white.

GUESS WORK

Go on! I say to the clouds, Move!
    As if my will could create currents
        powerful enough to force cumulus
            continents to cohere.

Edges of darkening masses
    are meant to interlock; merge
        and close the slowly narrowing gap
            right now.

Is that what I really want?
    The underlying layer of azure
        vanquished? The color that gives way
            to conjecture as I lean back in the swing?

We do not like uncertainty.
    Nature abhors a vacuum, scientists say, echoing
        Aristotle, as if insistence can calm the horrible
            suspense of emptiness we do not comprehend.

I, too, will die.
    But do I want to flesh out answers how and when;
        infuse the suffering genetic tests can predict
            into my limbs moving freely this spring afternoon?

To see the sky from the room where my dad waits,
    he would have to rise, balance
        by the window, bend down
            to look up beyond the courtyard walls.

Maybe he could, though he chooses
    to recline in the corner, gazing
        at a goldfinch alighting
            on a window feeder.

Or is it a flock
    taking turns?
        He never asks. Just smiles,
            his eyes a dazzling, unexpected blue.

SKY ATLAS

I wonder now, why did I shoot the sky
every day standing on a rise in the backyard,
arms raised, head lifted, moving
the camera ever so slightly;
scanning for clouds through the viewfinder,
compressing miles into millimeters, knowing
with each click, I was composing
something unreal
and gratifying?
It's been ten months
since my father's diagnosis.
I watch currents of clouds,
not the river that is yards from my tent,
and take them all in:
dense low cumulus rising
into towers and domes that suddenly distend
into bulging mounds;
stratocumulus unfurling
like white winding sheets;
heavy opaque cumulonimbus
that eventually must bear rain, sometimes
thunderstorms, hail, tornadoes, or maybe just virga.
Each cloud is a prayer,
condensing everything
I can't find the words for
into particles that no matter
how contradictory
stay aloft, held together by air.

CENTER OF GRAVITY

Romance (Style 2557) hangs on the closet door
in swirls of ruched organza, stays
of a sweetheart bodice; sixteen
satin buttons cinching
the waist of the fit-and-flare
silhouette my daughter will soon slip into

                              Peace of Mind rests on the desk:
                         a fax *To Whom It May Concern,*
                authorizing Darling-Fischer Family Mortuary
            to take his remains (embalmment, cremation, burial or
          refrigeration required within twenty-four hours) should
       my dad pass away while we travel to the ceremony abroad.

How hard it is to be the keeper of forms.

When I was pregnant,
I learned in class how to accommodate
the weight of an other:
    slow down;
        avoid quick changes;
            choose only
                smooth paths.

I could balance myself, each week my uterus expanding,
even as my center of gravity shifted up and back.

But *center of gravity* is:
    "an imaginary point in a body of matter,"
    says an encyclopedia of physics;
    a calculation valuable in designing bridges
    or predicting the behavior of a moving body.

Between the closet and the bed is
an expanse of sky blue wall

and five small oval mirrors, positioned
per an interior decorator at the store.

The asymmetry feels good.

                                      The fragmentation of my body, too:
                        knees reflected in the mirror hung low;
              elbow in another, higher, to the right;
      neck, near the highest.

I cannot see my face.

I know it is not immaterial.

                    ———

            What matters is the quickening
                in my chest, my belly, my gut
                      bending me

                                          into rays of light
                                              shimming

                    the frame of the door.

LAST RITES

Read it again, says my sister.

    I unsnap my wallet,
            touch the curled edge
                    of the index card with his words, and
                              pull it out from between dollar bills:

                                      I have to go. I may not be back.

                (What did the ticket say?) *To release me*

                      (hum of oxygen machine,
                      pitch rises with inhale,
                      dips with exhale)

She writes as I read.

How do I write what she says?

    So Dad knew?

        "Dad knew..."

"Dad knew—"
                      So Dad knew.

I don't know.

            ———

We are trying to make sense of our father's dying:

    not his death,
        expected sooner some days
            then later—
                for eighteen months, on hospice, off hospice, on,
                                              off, on—

        No, we are trying to make sense in the telling.

Death is the resolution
        that ends the suffering
                that was the conflict
                        for the dying.

For the surviving,[1]
        death is the ultimate absence:
                the wound that has no form, no
                matter to return to, to reach for, to
                move toward, to retell to

Dying is…
        an abstract object? subject of an objective dependent clause?

…the what separating us: father to daughter, daughter to sister, sister to sister.

"…the chaos narrative is probably the most embodied form of story," writes a medical sociologist. "…emotional battering is fundamental to chaos."[2]

                                  "The challenge is *to hear*"

Piles of yellow pads, steno pads, emails, phone messages—
I peel back pages delicately, phrases still tender to the touch

---

[1] Survive: from Latin *supervivere, super*—above + *vivere*—to live. (Five entries about Susan—a feminine name—in *Webster's New World Dictionary of the American Language*.)

[2] From *The Wounded Storyteller: Body, Illness, and Ethics* by Arthur w. Frank (1995). His claim that a wounded body is a call to story is not new. Teiresias, the blind Theban in Greek mythology, was keenly perceptive, prophesized to generations of kings and heroes who failed to listen. "[L]isteners," Frank says, "have trouble facing what is being said as a possibility or a reality in their own lives."

Mr. Buck, he said he had a message
to lay flat on the bed, no pillow,
with his legs out straight
and his hands crossed over his chest.
He says, I have to stay this way
for seven hours to be healed.

Hello Susan!

Just to give you an update regarding your dad:

-he is eating and drinking less, Henry feeds him lately but sometimes your dad does not want to be fed.
- i take his mid arm circumference as my reference to see if he is losing weight, today's measurement is 23 cm on right arm, it decreased to 0.5 CM in 2 wks. his cheek bones are more prominent.
- he is sleeping more in day time
- he is less engaged
- his coughing comes and goes, i got an order for breathing treatment every 6 hrs.
- he is more incontinent as well, he has no bowel and bladder control most of the time now.
- vital signs still with normal ranges so far.

Dear Susan, I was pretty concerned about your dad's condition. He was in the chair but in a fetal position. Henry and I tried talking and I kept touching his hands and face. We did the best we could to sit him up and loosen his hands.

Hello!
He really declined for the past 2 weeks, he is not imminent yet but for me it is better for you to visit him as you can while he can still talk and while he can still recognize you.

Sunday
    I offer to massage your shoulders—you don't refuse—
    I run my hands that look exactly like yours

  down your back, outline your scapula—
    "wing bones," my mother-in-law used to call them—

You tell me: *I'm waiting to be picked up today. They're going to ask me about the car that was in an accident. It was a mess, a woman had been murdered in there. I had to clean it up. Then there was the kidnapping…They'll put a line in here, in my arm, cut up to here, a slit, then turn me over onto my back. Oh, there's more.*
    That sounds like a nightmare.
    No, it's real.

I want to end my life.
    (Were those his exact words? Why can't I remember?)

The chaos narrative has no coherent sequence.[3]

---

triangle of skin at his neck showing
blue pjs with navy piping—
  no wrinkles—
    skin younger than mine in morning light

The triangle, I keep coming back to it…

"The ancient Roman physician Quintus Serenus Sammonicus," I tell medical students, "prescribed a triangular piece of parchment inscribed at the top with ABRACADABRA to be worn around the neck. The words filled the paper. Each descending line dropped a letter, funneling the healing rhythm into the patient's body as the word disappears."

      If only I could force the paranoia
        to drain from his body—
          bring him peace

---

[3] "The voice that might express deepest chaos is subsumed in interruptions…" (Frank).

> I want to hold you & hug you
> but ~~I don~~ I ~~kn~~
> That's not enough

"What language shall I borrow…?"

On Palm Sunday, I make notes on the back of the prayer card:

> *from "O Sacred Head, Now Wounded"*[4]
> *Text, Latin 12-13th century*
> *Music, Bach 1729*

I do not follow instructions.
I do not pass the card to the usher at the center aisle.

I tuck it inside my wallet.

All week I listen, hoping
> as I unfold the card to release
> > the passion into a tongue
> > > I can understand.

We sang together, Dad and me, unexpectedly
Valentine's Day when members of his church
visited the skilled nursing center.

Swallowing had been so hard that morning,
little bites of scrambled eggs, even coffee
choking him until he gasped, his face purple.

---

[4] Translated into English in the 19th century by a Presbyterian minister, the hymn is based on a Latin poem attributed to Arnulf Leuven. Each verse addresses a different member of Jesus's body as he hangs on the cross.

But he hummed. I held the sheet music,
"O the Deep, Deep Love of Jesus,"
leaning over the arm of the wheelchair

so he could see. My cheek grazed
the shoulder of his gray wool jacket.
His voice joined mine: "Leading onward,

leading homeward,
To my glorious
rest above—"

a trembling soprano and frail tenor
(though he knew the words
by heart).

———

Dad knew.
We all know how it ends.

    Or how it *will*

        Therein is the mystery:

that indistinguishable unnamable flash of time[5]
when a micro-second shifts, when
will transmutes the body and
tenses change the future into the present that
is and *is not* as perfect as

---

[5]Planck time? Theoretical physicists estimate it is an infinitesimal 5.39×10^{44} seconds, the smallest measurement of time possible, though it has few, if any, practical applications.

> what it felt like in our bodies:
> the past that has passed
> into holiness.

"...*only say the word and I shall be healed.*"

———

I don't say anything,
my eyes closed, arms splayed
over the red damask spread over
the body that was my dad.

You'll see only his face from the neck up,
the funeral director had explained to my sister
who dropped me off for the private viewing.
You'll be allowed one hour...

I caress his face, a hint of powder
on his cheek, perhaps blush
or the glow of candles flickering
in red globes.

His skin is cool; my cheek, too,
as I rest on the layer of ice packs:
protection against time
belied by tissues I've wadded

strewn on the carpet
like white petals. I touch
his cheek, the pale skin under
his eye, his ear lobe.

His flesh yields to my fingers
and I to the breadth of his chest.
So strong, so secure, I whispered
to him during our last living

embrace, although I'm amazed
at how peaceful we are
in death's. I stand up slowly,
comb my fingers through his white hair,

tuck a strand behind his ear
and kiss his forehead.
Then I mouth
the only words

that matter now,
or ever, and exhale.
Under the damask, I slide a letter
and leave.

———

Your Legacy, my sister wrote at the top of the page
ripped from her journal when Dad said, "Please…write that down…."
Her memory of a blessing I'd said
for him twenty-five years ago.
Remember the dedication? I remind him on the phone
when she tells me what he asked her to write;
Your granddaughter wrote to you in her thesis?
Write that, too, he says to my sister,
and she does, adding her own
and another, long-distance from my older daughter.

And then,
my sister tells me, once again, how
Dad folded the paper and
held it to his chest.

ASCENSION

White sheet wound around
        his neck like an ascot
                for the viewing

unfurls as he ascends
        until all I can see of my dad
                are the flats of his feet

no longer chafed
        and chapped but
                resplendent:

resoled in gem stones
        dazzling as sunlit sea
                and sky. Even his heart

I imagined deep, dark red
        has cooled to azure as it
                disintegrates on re-entry:

glittery particles of lapis
        catching
                at the back of my throat—

                    ……

I'm under house arrest,
        he would tell me, lodged
                in his recliner. Twisting

in the loveseat, I'd turn
        to face his shrunken body,
                my own so sore

sitting for hours.
        We are both, I'd think,
                trapped in the bone-house.

I let the Old Norse kenning
    release my mind
        into paradox

that two months later
    shapeshifts into another:
        How can I love you without

remembering the lighthouse
    of my childscape,
        lantern-keeper, beam-sweeper, bell-ringer

anklets of memories
    shackling you
        to the *ban-hus* of my living?

        ......

Long peasant dress, over-shirt,
    sweater and skirt: I've bought all
        in shades of sapphire

since you died, though
    I can't seem to slip my arms
        through the sleeves.

I'm afraid my shoulders
    will sag if I let
        what I heard you say

about *love* linger;
    I will suffer
        the fine dust of lapis

into my body,
    exploding every
        daughter cell

beyond the spectrum
      into radiance exhilarating
            as God's-candle.

CHROMATICS

On the seventh day after we buried my dad,
                                                        a new shade of blue
            (though material scientists discovered it eight years before:
            the year my dad was diagnosed with non-Hodgins lymphoma,
            his third cancer; my mother, a rare form of lupus disabling her
                                                      central nervous system).

The "serendipitous discovery" of a new blue, "a happy accident," came to light the day Crayola announced a contest to name the color.

From 90,000 submissions, five finalists:
    __ *Dreams Come Blue*
    __ *Bluetiful*
    __ *Blue Moon Bliss*
    __ *Reach for the Stars*
    __ *Star Bangled Blue*

Five months after my dad's diagnosis, my parents moved into a retirement center.
    He: excited, relieved, in remission
    She: resistant, confused, dying
    We: my sister and I boxed
              their antique flow blue china,
                  blue onion dishes,
                          blue crystal champagne flutes—

Blue is inadequate.

The new hue is technically *YInMn*.
    (Mix yttrium, indium, and manganese
    with oxygen, heat in a furnace to 2,000 degrees;
    the elements form a vibrant non-toxic pigment.)

"Children will be able to colour the sky a different shade for the first time in 200 years": the lead article in *The Telegraph*'s science section.

In 1802, a French chemist discovered the pigment for cobalt blue. Crayola made the first cobalt blue crayon in 1903. Four other shades were included in the original box of 38 crayons. Red, though, was the prominent color with eight variations for children to choose from.

Production of cobalt blue stopped in 1958.

The color is officially *retired*.

(*Retire*: to take out of circulation)

Fourteen other shades are retired, including:

Teal Blue	Aquamarine
Light Blue	Cerulean Blue
Middle Blue	Green Blue
Maximum Blue	Blue I
Ultramarine	Blue II

Three shades of red were retired after seven years: *Permanent Geranium Lake, Dark Venetian Red,* and *Light Venetian Red*. Three decades later when the company opted for simpler names, *English Vermillion* and *Madder Lake* were taken out of circulation. *Brick Red, Scarlet, Dark Red,* and *Orange Red* were added.

When the marketing director asked my dad why he hadn't considered moving into the retirement center earlier, he said: "I was waiting to get old."

He was eighty-six and not retired.

(*Retired*: withdrawn or apart from the world; in seclusion)

He'd twice retired
        then re-entered the job force.
I found business cards
        among his effects:

M.E. Sample and Associates
Private Investigations

M.E. (Buck) Sample
TRAVEL CONSULTANT
Travel Advisors of _____

Crayola continued producing three shades of blue under new names:

> *Midnight Blue*—"Known as 'Prussian Blue,' 1903-1958."
> *Blue-Violet*—"Known as 'Violet,' 1949-1958."
> *Blue-Green*—"Known as 'Middle Blue-Green,' 1949-1958."

New residents are encouraged to wear name-tags at the retirement center, which promises on its website:
> You'll be surrounded by fascinating people from all walks of life.
> > You'll relax...
> > > You'll delight...
> > > > You'll enjoy...
> > > > > You'll live life the way it's meant to be lived.

Celestial blue is an anomaly.

The color was produced from 1903 to circa 1910.
It is the only shade of blue in the company's history without an end date.

Promotional material assures residents a comprehensive continuum of care
> (On another page:
> "...should their health care needs change.")

"What is amazing," said the material scientist, "is that through much of human history, civilizations around the world have sought inorganic compounds that could be used to paint things but often had limited success."

"The YInMn blue pigment is very stable/durable. There is no change in the color when exposed to high temperatures, water, mildly acidic and alkali conditions."

Every news article about the discovery repeats: *The new color will not fade.*
        (*Fade*: to dim; to lose strength; to disappear; to die out)

———

On a June night after my dad had died,
I waited with my husband for the full moon,
    the *Strawberry Moon,*
        to rise.

We sat on a porch in the red rock desert,
peering east through branches of pinyon pine.
    Why could I still see
        a wide band of blue
            after the sun had set?

Moving his hand
    through the hot still air,
        my husband separated his fingers:
            Imagine a prism
                permitting only certain wavelengths
                    to pass through the atmosphere—

The origin of a color
not found in the earth depends
"on the intricate arrangements of atoms,"
explained the material scientist.

                        (*Blue* is inorganic,
              not derived from a living organism.)

Ancient Egyptians
    prized the semi-precious
        lapis lazuli,

mining and grinding,
    mixing and heating
        until a blue hue

appeared, so expensive
    it was reserved for royalty
        and remained largely

uncommon,
    thus unnamed
        (our words linked to sight).

That night,
filtered through the desert atmosphere:

    Dad's arms outstretched,
        reaching up   rigid
           in the air-conditioned hospital room;

fingers cramping,
        curling,
    grotesque as he
           strained.

I want you to help me see…
He reaches for the temple of my eyeglasses.

"He's delirious," says the retirement center executive director.
"I've been a nurse. I know delirium."
        (She does not want him to return to his apartment).

We do not want him to return to the *health center*—
    known as "skilled nursing facility," 2005-present;
        "nursing home," 1950-1970s;
        "Odd Fellows Home," 1912- circa 1999

        —where he was said to have had an "incident."

        (When someone is found on the floor
           beside his bed, bleeding,
        the ER doctor tells me, it's a *fall*.)

I (try to) tell the director:
>When someone is told he must move from "independent living" to "assisted living," he is likely to be upset.
>When he awakes in the dark, using words more forcefully than ever before, he is undoubtedly distraught.

What do you see, Dad?

Red, red...not like a rose.
A fire. It's hot. It hurts.
Hell—Hell, hell...
>(To age successfully: "feeling healthier, happier, and more fulfilled in mind, body, and spirit"
>—retirement center website)

I have to struggle—
>his tone, unfamiliar.

>*Call the nurse. Now!*
>*Get me water! I need water—*
>*Why can't you...*

You're just like all the rest. I thought you'd be different.

I'm doing the best I can, Dad.

Well, it's not good enough...

On the plane, I read the words of a Swiss psychotherapist: "'Delirious' often means incomprehensible and without dignity." Her work has just been translated into English: "... symbolic language assigns meaning to the utterances and communication of the dying and affords us an opportunity to empathize with them."

Red is aggressive, assertive, determined
Red is rage, anger, danger
Red is longing, love
Red is blood

I wrap my hands around his,
    reaching higher as he does:
        our fingers, the shape
            of our knuckles, nail beds
                ("Oh Buck, she has your hands!"
                    in a another hospital
                    in another time)
        indistinguishable.

———

I said hurtful things to you yesterday—
    His right hand holds mine,
        squeezing it rhythmically
            like a heartbeat.

People in our family—Dad, Mother, Duane, Esther—died suddenly:
    heart attack, stroke—
        the skin where the IV had been taped, raw and red—
        I'm not afraid of dying.

Later, I will write in my notebook:

This is a visit in shades of red:
    Red bare heels hanging over the edge of the mattress
    Red stains from tomato soup on his gown
    Red face and ears when he chokes

I wear my black cardigan
    and a pendant with a red stone
        …

I will not finish.

Red is as inadequate as blue.

———

    Unstrung, the bloodstone
            remains in my dresser
                in a small well
                    lined with fabric
                        the same shade of red
                            as the velour bag
                                that held the urn
                          holding what had been my dad
                                that I carried
                              to the cemetery.
                        I wore blue opal earrings,
                  a scarf in shimmering
            shades of blue as if I could absorb
          his death; experience some
        unsayable blue seeping
      through my skin,
    so I can imagine the words
      for my living his dying
        that begin the telling
of my own:

AFTER BLUE

I gaze at his recliner, still
extended when I return:
    white towel bunched
        where his back had been;
            another on the seat, rippled
                with his final movements.

A wadded tissue on the carpet;
    blue emetic bowl on the windowsill;
        eyeglasses folded, lens smudged,
            chapstick uncapped on the bedside table.

I take photos with my phone,
moving around the assisted living apartment:
    empty bag of peanut butter candy;
        packaged alcohol prep pads;
            diapers in the closet,
                stacks of applesauce cups;
                    Valentine pinned to the wall,
                      edges of the doily curling
                        in toward *Be Mine.*

    Still life, I tell myself, focusing
    on two blue cups and a spoon in the sink.

                    Ancient Greeks knew where
            "the human eye loves to view subjects":
                    off-center, never
                            in the middle.

                    Photographers still look to the
                      Golden Rule of Thirds.

In the final photo, my eye makes out
    the shadow near the drain:

        How the deep blue of the glass
shines on stainless steel
      in the lower right quadrant.

                                But where the lines cross
                                      at *nought*, as in:
                                    indentations,
                          empty bag,
                                  clothesless hanger…

              ———

                                  …unless I am seeing,
                                        months later,
                          not the minutiae of a life spent—
                                  but
              a presence
                    in the stillness:

                          a human subject neither
              my dad
                      nor me, holding the camera:
                              but something—

                  evanescent

                      as breath,

        inaudible
     as waves of sound
             composing

soft tissues of a
    life, still
        taking shape within the body
            of my daughter.

I've studied the strip of images she left
    in her childhood bedroom:

                      mottled
              head and belly,

                              wisps of legs

                                      blurry shapes in gray,
                             providing no insight

                                      into what it will feel like
                            to behold
                                            who comes
                                            into being
                                                    next.

                                            Eyes
                                  are indecipherable
                                in the sonogram,

                                              drawing mine

                        into the pure black of the

            background:
                    absent
                                  of echoes

                              and the pressure of logic.

                                    Keats named
                  our human quality of

"...being in uncertainties,
    mysteries, doubt..."
                                      Negative Capability

>   *dwell in Possibility,*
>   I tell medical students
>   the first day we meet in
>   INTMD 7992, "Writing the Doctor-Patient Relationship":

    bury

          (temporarily)

                scientific confidence;

disarm yourselves with doubt
      in shades
            darkening patients' lives.

> *To learn the transport of pain,*
> *As blind men learn the sun;*
> ...
>
> *This is the sovereign anguish,*
> *This, the signal woe!*
> *These are the patient laureates...*

                    We read so many,
              patient and impatient;

            listen to the imprint
                of their voices,

        black on white,
          I forget

                just how much
                  I (mis)trust

prominence:

                                    how it overshadows,
                                         oversimplifies

                Possibility

---

      happening right now between
the dynamism of tiny white belly and brain,

            painful emptiness of space
            in images of life, still

            developing in the mid-tones
            of my body—graying hair,

              skin mottled, wrinkled
              on the back of my hands—

            yes, taking shape in lines
             crisscrossing my palms:

          crosshatchings that deepen
          as my fingers come together,

                  cupping
                  all I know

                  and don't
                  of love.

Susan Sample holds a unique position at the University of Utah in Salt Lake City. She is the writer-in-residence at Huntsman Cancer Institute where she guides patients and family members, physicians, nurses, and staff in writing about their experiences with illness and disease. In the School of Medicine, she is a faculty member in the Program in Medical Ethics and Humanities, Department of Internal Medicine, where she teaches reflective writing and medical humanities to medical students, residents, and physicians. She advises the Physicians Literature & Medicine Discussion Group and the medical student literary magazine, *Rubor: Reflections on Medicine from the Wasatch Front*. In the College of Humanities, she teaches in the Department of Writing and Rhetoric Studies, focusing on the diversity of discourses that compose health and medicine.

She holds a BA in philosophy from Whitman College, an MFA in creative writing from the University of Arizona, and a PhD in communication with emphases in rhetoric and narrative in medicine from the University of Utah. Her poetry has won awards from the Utah Arts Council, *Crab Creek Review*, and *Writer's Digest*. One of her poems was selected by Paul Muldoon for the 2018 Shirley McClure Poetry Contest at the Irish Arts & Writers Festival. Her poetry has appeared in journals, including: *Tupelo Quarterly, Intima: A Journal of Narrative Medicine, The Healing Muse: A Journal of Literary and Visual Arts, The Sow's Ear Poetry Review, ellipsis,* and *Salt Flats Annual*. Her first chapbook, *Terrible Grace,* was published by Finishing Line Press in 2011.